LEVEL
1
AGES 5 AND 6

SHARKS

BRENDA Z. GUIBERSON

SCHOLASTIC
REFERENCE

PHOTO CREDITS: Cover: James D. Watt/Innerspace Visions. Page 1: Fred McConnaughey/ Photo Researchers, Inc.; 3: Gregory Ochocki/Photo Researchers, Inc.; 4: Gwen Lowe/Innerspace Visions; 5: Norbert Wu/Peter Arnold, Inc.; 6: Norbert Wu/Peter Arnold, Inc.; 7: Tom McHugh/Photo Researchers, Inc.; 8: Steinhart Aquarium/ Tom McHugh/Photo Researchers, Inc.; 9 (top): Makoto Kubo/ Innerspace Visions; 9 (bottom): Tom McHugh/Photo Researchers, Inc.; 10: James D. Watt/ Innerspace Visions; 11: Howard Hall/Innerspace Visions; 12: Bruce Rasner/ Innerspace Visions; 13: Andrew Syred/Science Photo Library/Photo Researchers, Inc.; 14: Mark Conlin/Innerspace Visions; 15: Edward R. Degginger/Bruce Coleman Inc.; 16: Fred Bavendam/Peter Arnold, Inc.; 17: Gerard Soury/Peter Arnold, Inc.; 18: Fred Bavendam/Peter Arnold, Inc.; 19: S.J. Krasemann/Peter Arnold, Inc.; 20: Ferrari/Watt/Innerspace Visions; 21: A.&A. Ferrari/Innerspace Visions; 22: Florian Graner/Innerspace Visions; 23: Jeff Rotman/Innerspace Visions; 24: Jeffrey L. Rotman/Peter Arnold, Inc.; 25: Gregory Ochocki/Photo Researchers, Inc.; 26, 27: Doug Perrine/Innerspace Visions; 28: Ron & Valerie Taylor/Bruce Coleman Inc.; 29: Fred McConnaughey/Photo Researchers, Inc.; 30: C.C. Lockwood/Bruce Coleman Inc.

ISBN 0-439-26985-7

Book design by Barbara Balch and Kay Petronio
Photo research by Sarah Longacre

10 9 8 7 6 5 4 3 2 1   02 03 04 05 06

Printed in the U.S.A. 23

First printing, May 2002

We are grateful to Francie Alexander, reading specialist, and
to Adele M. Brodkin, Ph.D., developmental psychologist,
for their contributions to the development of this series.

Our thanks also to our science consultant Lisa Mielke, Assistant Director
of Education, Aquarium for Wildlife Conservation, Brooklyn, New York.

Sharks are amazing fish. They live in oceans all around the world. Some like warm water. Others like cold water. A few sharks can even live in rivers.

Some sharks are as big
as school buses. Other sharks
are as small as pencils.

Fast sharks can speed
around the ocean. Slow
ones hide in the sand.

Sharks have lots of teeth.
But they do not have bones.

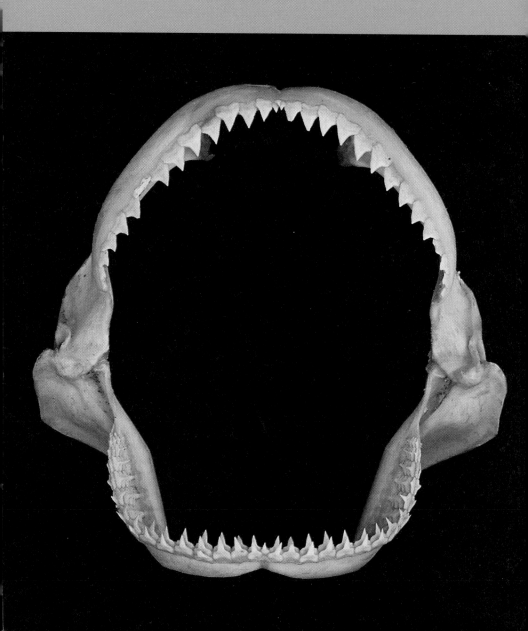

Take a Closer Look

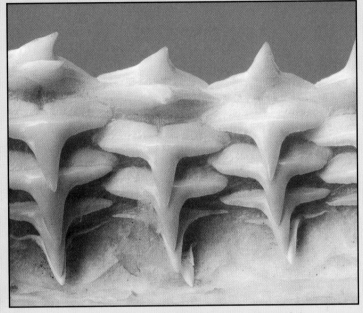

Grey reef sharks have lots of teeth!

The skeleton of a shark is made of **cartilage** (**kar**-tuh-lij).

Let's take a close look at
a few sharks.

leopard shark

saw shark

bonnethead shark

The great white shark is
fast and strong. It has big
teeth that tear and cut.

The basking shark has a big mouth. But it has tiny teeth the size of little seeds. This shark cannot bite into big things. As water flows through its mouth, the shark strains out tiny plants and animals that it eats.

Few people have ever seen
the megamouth shark. It was
not discovered until 1976.

No one knows much about the megamouth shark. It has flabby skin, a big, glowing mouth, and tiny teeth. The megamouth cannot catch big things. It eats tiny plants and animals, like the basking shark does.

Take a Closer Look

*A close-up of tiny animals
that megamouth sharks eat*

Baby sharks can take care of themselves. Some hatch from eggs. The eggs are protected in egg cases.

Other sharks grow inside the mother before they are born. When sharks are little, sometimes big fish eat them.

A baby shark comes out of its egg case.

Baby sharks are called **pups**. Some shark pups have special colors to help them hide. Colors for hiding are called **camouflage** (**kam**-uh-flahz).

Baby leopard sharks have spots. They hide near rocks and sea grasses. Their colors help them hide.

The wobbegong (**woh**-buh-gong) shark is flat and slow. To catch something to eat, it must hide and wait.

The wobbegong has spots. It has skin flaps that wave like seaweed. Because it looks like sand and seaweed, the wobbegong has great camouflage.

The horn shark has a pig-like snout and teeth that crush and crunch. With its big snout, it sniffs out clams hiding in the sand. The shark's teeth crunch through hard clamshells.

Sometimes the horn shark eats purple **sea urchins** (**sea ur**-chinz). The urchins leave a purple stain on the shark's teeth.

The thresher shark is smooth and fast. It has a long tail that whips through the water.

A thresher shark's tail can slap and slash other fish. The fish are knocked out and easy to catch.

The lanternshark lives deep in the ocean where it is dark. It has large eyes to help it see. It also glows with its own green light, just like a firefly does.

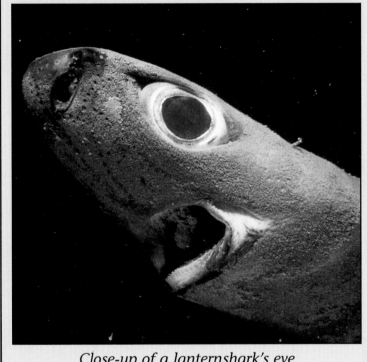

Close-up of a lanternshark's eye

Lanternsharks are small but they eat big squid. They may hunt in packs to catch them.

23

The hammerhead shark
has a head like a hammer. It
swings its wide head to find
stingrays buried in the sand.

Stingrays have sharp **barbs** in their tails. Some kinds of hammerheads have barbs stuck in their mouths because stingrays fight back.

There are over 350 different kinds of sharks. Every year we discover new ones. Sharks have survived for 400 million years.

Some sharks lived before
the time of the dinosaurs. The
dinosaurs are extinct (ek-**stingkt**)
but sharks still survive.

Today, some sharks are in trouble. Every year, millions and millions of them are killed by humans. Shark **fins** are used for soup. Sharkskin is used for clothing.

Some sharks are killed
because humans are afraid
of them.

Sharks are ocean experts.
Over millions of years, they have
developed the skills to survive.
They are important to all life
around them. Some of these
amazing fish need our protection.

Glossary

barbs—sharp, stinging spines on the tails of some rays

camouflage (**kam**-uh-flahz)—colors and textures that help animals hide

cartilage (**kar**-tuh-lij)—tough, elastic material that forms the skeletons of sharks and part of the nose and ears of humans

fins—winglike parts of fish used to swim, steer, and balance

pups—baby sharks

sea urchins (**sea ur**-chinz)—round animals with a hard shell covered with long, movable spines

stingrays—flat fish that have long thin tails with barbs that sting

A Note to Parents

Learning to read is such an exciting time in a child's life. You may delight in sharing your favorite fairy tales and picture books with your child.

But don't forget the importance of introducing your child to the world of nonfiction. The ability to read and comprehend factual material will be essential to your child in school, and throughout life. The Scholastic Science Readers™ series was created especially with beginning readers in mind. These books, with their clear texts and beautiful photographs, will help you to share the wonders of science with *your* new reader.

Suggested Activity

The best (and safest!) way to see live sharks is at an aquarium. If there is an aquarium near you, call and see if they have a shark exhibit. The National Aquarium in Baltimore, Maryland, has two exhibits featuring sharks. You can pet a baby nurse shark at the Aquarium of the Americas in New Orleans, Louisiana, which has one of the world's largest shark collections. And, at the Newport Aquarium in Newport, Kentucky, you can have a real underwater shark adventure. The Surrounded by Sharks exhibit features a see-through plastic tunnel so visitors can watch sharks all around them. There is even a see-through section of flooring. Look at your feet, and you may see a shark looking back at you!